INK BLOT IN
A POET'S BLOODSTREAM

Heather Angelika Dooley

All rights reserved. No part of this book may be reproduced, stored, or transmitted by any means, whether auditory, graphic, mechanical, or electronic without written permission of both publisher and author, except in the case of brief excerpts used in critical articles and reviews. Unauthorized reproduction of any part of this work is illegal and is punishable by law.

ISBN 1-944662-35-6

Publishing date: May 2019

Cover Design by Mike Quiñones G

Dedication

Dedicated to my husband and Cowboy: Sean Donal Pecor.

Even though these words are from bygone times,
he reminds me every day that he truly was the only person that
kept me so alive that I didn't have time to write poetry about him.
I thank my lucky stars every day that nothing else ever worked out—
and that because of destiny, I always stayed pointed at Polaris
(even with all of my creatively paused, misused ellipses).

Credits:

To those others who help me push the creativity from my heart through my veins:

Wilhelmina Indigo Dooley—my magician musician who inspires me with her natural flows of artistry and has become my biggest muse. This happened the day that she opened her eyes for the first time and showed me my new world through them. Everything became more poetic then. I fed her with the veins that she now feeds me through, every day. She is the love of my life.

Chloe Louise Pecor—my *Tigger* whose infectious honest-to-goodness makes everyone around her want to bounce—another lover of poetry and wholehearted words. A writing brawler with the toughest kind heart out there… She will bolster you when life tries to bully you because her love is a buoy. She's the real deal beacon of buoyancy. She does not know what a present to the world that this is yet, but I do.

Heather Angelika Dooley

Moira Kathryn Pecor—my emotional *twinsie*. She is one of my favorite feminist swans. Sometimes life makes you think that there are no accidents; we came into each other's lives right at the right time. Her journey is an inspiration to me every day, and we traveled down so many of the same roads decades apart from the other. Her beauty comes in the form of truth, honesty, bravery, instinct, and, most of all, grace. She is a graceful metamorphosis.

Garrick Alexander Pecor—my confident and charismatic conversationalist; so few people can capture my interest long enough to talk as much as me. He has a tough exterior to a lot of people, but he is one of the gentlest souls that I have ever known, deep down in the recesses of the things that he cannot undo and undoes every day in his brilliant way. He is the son that I was given as a gift for always wanting one.

Amelia Jordan Pecor—my precious peanut, my granddaughter, my spunky and plucky Amelia Bedelia. Her Mommy and Daddy brought so much more expressiveness to my Nonnie Library. She will fillip more freedom in her Nonnie's imagination, every day, as I watch hers unfold. Youth brings young life into everything that you do, and her young life has refreshed us all.

Ink Blot in a Poet's Bloodstream

Nancy Lynn Huffman—my first editor in life; my *Little Engine that Could*. She printed my first page by bringing me into this book of life. If you're lucky, mothers are your first love, your first friend, and your first editors, until you learn to edit for yourself. I was one of the lucky ones. If you're REALLY lucky, these things never change. I am here to say that I am REALLY lucky.

Robert Gonzalez—my Bobster, our Powpow, my dad. Genetically, I had a father. Through love, I got a dad. This is the man who sends me cards, wants to hear what I have to say about the world, supports all of my passions, and shows up and arrives for me. That's a dad to me. I cherish him. And above and beyond being the dad that I always deserved, he is the best damn Powpow to my daughter than any child could ask for. She only has one. If I didn't love the tar out of him enough before her, I couldn't love the tar out of him more than I have over the last 15 years.

Hazel Theresa Pecor—my mother-in-law who reads tea leafs, loves psychic mediums, and has become one of my dearest friends outside of being another mother figure in my life. She supports me in every way, as another empathic feeler and eccentric. As she always says, "Oh, that's the way it goes, Tu's (*deuce*). I am so happy that we got you. I prayed for you to come every day. My son smiles again!" I am so happy that I got her, too; she gave me the son who makes me smile again, just the same.

Also, my beloved extended family, whose love surpasses time lapses and distance—
Diane Scott, John Scott, Brent Scott, Cris Scott, Abbi Scott, and Ryan Scott.

Finally, my book team—

my publisher, Drew Becker, my editors, Trudy Grenon Stoddert and Gordon MacLaclan, my cover artist, Mike Quiñones G, my forward by author and poet, Merrit Malloy, and my graphic designer, Nadia Martin.

Without any of you, this book would be an impossible possibility.

I thank you all for rallying for me in this pep rally of poetry that needed other hands on it after mine had it to hand over.

I have always said that my books are children that I have given birth to and have to set free to the world to be their own people. Well, it takes a village. Thanks for being my vigilant village.

#MadRespect and #Gratitude

Contents

Dedication iii

Credits: iv

Foreward xv

I Live to Right; I Write to Live 1

R.S.V.P. 2

Hunger of Love 3

A Very Cold Day 4

Spring Cleaning 5

The Truth Speaks in Volumes 8

Essential Elements 9

The *I'm Through* Haiku 10

The Mermaid and the Mariner 11

Everyone's One True Love 15

Laughter Should Always Be Reckless Abandonment ... 16

Abracadabra 18

Invaluable Lessons 20

Writer/Lover Confidentiality 21

Spot Healing Tool 22

Prelude to an Open Door 23

Final Eternal Sunshine 25

We All Move Out and Move On 26

Deadbolt 28

Frozen Food 29

Lilies 31

Unfair Taxi Fare 33

Last Christmas' Poinsettias 34

He's Charcoal Now 36

Featherweight 39

Opalescent Beetle on Her Back 40

Mileage 44

A (Wo)Man of Sixty Winters 45

Nobody Walkies the Talkies Anymore 47

Slumberland 49

When a Bolt Bolts 50

Joyride 51

These Germs Aren't for Pirates 52

The Gateway 54

Keeping It All Inside 55

I Love With Kerosene 57

In the Dark 59

Gut	62
Streetlamps	63
Double Dutch	65
Transient Heart Surfer	66
Rib Cage Cell	68
Don't Knock It 'Til You Try It. Twice	70
The Urn I Earned but Never Deserved	71
Keys to Life	73
Independence's Place	74
Your Voodoo Doll Baby	77
Venus Verses Neptune	78
The Final Master*peace* Always Says Hers	80
Natural Disaster	82
Imprinted in 2010	85
Phantom	86
Window of Opportunity	87
Foreclosed Heart	89
That's Heaven	91
Rough Draft	92
There Is Only One Second Half	94
Changing Reasons	96

Manumit 97

A Foreigner on Cloud Nine 98

Plugged in Unplugged 100

Women in the Cabinet 101

Stay-at-Homeless Mom 102

His-story 104

The Whole Package 106

Dream Catcher 107

I Was Taught to Slay Dragons 110

Teardrop Dance 112

A Logbook of Limbo 113

Still and All 115

Table d'hôte 117

I Forgot My Keys and Locked Myself Out of Me 118

A Vow Forever New 120

Sleep Tight on Your Right Side of the Bed 121

You Can't Make Memories in Messenger 123

Palette Clean 124

Simplicity Is Best 126

Loose Ends 127

Divided in Two 131

Robotic Thrombotic	131
Beach Winters	133
Rendered Speechless	136
Killing Time	137
Penitentiary Perfection	139
Sanctity	142
Even Fireflies Fade Out Sometimes	143
Insufficient Postage	148
Your Largest Organ	149
It's Funny Who Chimes In	150
Cleaning Out Underneath the Couch	152
I've Learned Nothing is Really Waterproof	154
Let's Just Pretend	156
No Better Half	157
"Tom"	158
Love Is Blind	166
Now I'm a Blond	167
One in the Same	170
Sometimes the Quiet Ones Say the Most	171
The Kiss I Use	173
Root Words	176

Dot, Dot, Dot 177

Upper Resuscitation Infection 179

Berlin Has Nothing On Us 180

Honest Evidence 181

Going to Confession 183

Weathered Over Time 185

Finishing Last Isn't a Bad Thing 186

Manner of the Love Chapel 187

Enlarged Heart 188

First Snow 189

Don't Let it Get Stuck on the Way Out 190

Lye Soap 191

Trapeze Artist—This Is My Arial Act 192

Back Pocket 193

Dear John Done, ... 196

Make Love to Your Life 198

Let's Just Get This Out of the Way Now 201

The Vow To My Next Book 202

Foreward

This is Heather Angelika Dooley's best work ever. It multiplies her. She has created another body of work that is so touching, and so delicately an honest meditation of life, love and consciousness. Lovers of Dooley will feel her real ink blots bleeding through the poetic passion of her bloodstream streaming from her warm, humane and patient heart to the page.

—Merrit Malloy, *Writers Guild of America Award for Television: Anthology Original* & Poet

Ink Blot in a Poet's Bloodstream

I Live to Right; I Write to Live

He asked,

    "So, you had another book in you?"

I replied,

    "The day that I don't, I die."

This entitlement could be my new title for the next…
    (I have no other choice but to) release.

Maybe, just maybe, if I keep my points pointed at Polaris,
    and keep making those wishes every night:

    Starlight, star bright, first star I see tonight…?

Who needs a compass when
you live to right with such a straight-shooting star in hand?

Here's to release…

R.S.V.P.

Things always show up

    when they don't arrive.

Hunger of Love

His buttery words
melted against my toasty skin,
like honeyed icing on a pastry
fresh out of the oven.

His lips on mine
sent a dash of lime straight to my thighs—
his tongue tasting my thoughts
with a tangerine twist, full of zest.

His hot and bothered body of sweat
felt refreshing against my flesh,
like the water beads on a frosty Mason jar of lemonade
the summer of my first brush with self-rule and release,

even though it was February.

A Very Cold Day

You are my fireplace,

    and I am your kindling…

        your *tinder*.

Together we're a flame,

    because we just…

        (light a) match.

Spring Cleaning

1.

A little bit of spring
came to greet me at the back door,
as if I were its new neighbor,
with a homemade, warm apple pie
in her hand—
a forceful fog rising,
like steam and dough.

Wouldn't you know that
I never left, even when I was gone.
I might have been buried deep,
but I had become the most shallow
of seeds, scattering.
It takes quite a bit of rain and snow
to grow through that toughest layer
of top dirt.

2.

A blindingly red cardinal
and a keg breasted robin
chirruped their winter stories
from a branch to a power line
about where the earthworms
would be resurfacing.

Even in enemy fields,
we all come out of the frozen mud
to get a peep of what could bloom
...soon, if we let it.
In the dark, hours melt into days,
but in the scintillating light
we fight like we're in a Punic War.

3.

I collected metaphors
and carried them in,
inside my pocket,
for my pen to play with
on paper, in order to not
make a mess, like
my daughter plays with
Moon Sand on newspaper.
I didn't want to sweep up
my wholehearted feelings
on this halfhearted, rousing day.

4.

He helped me clean out my head
in time for floweret sunshine,
while I raked dead leaves from
underneath the bed of my nails
that were waiting to be organized in diaries.
As the *Forbidding Numb* piled up,

he laundered my abandoned hope clean.
All that I could smell on my hands were
the roots of the root words I had diluted with
extra letters and slushiness.

5.

There isn't a corner that we missed;
and, in no time at all,
I will forget the wretchedness of *this* winter.

Soon, I will only smell peonies and calla lilies,
fresh cotton sheets, and maybe—just maybe—
the paperless books that I have written
being pressed like petals;
yet, no longer incinerators burning
perished wood that already
pushed up daisies
right when autumn left its leaves
behind me.

The Truth Speaks in Volumes

I know that I should never write a whole manuscript in one day,
        but I could.

It is hard to look back…
        …on all that you remembered…
           …to forget.

Essential Elements

I told him how
the one before
told me that I was
    his addiction—
that "he" thirsted for,
trembled for,
and found me to be a habit too hard to break.

He told me,
"He had it all wrong.
You should have been
    his oxygen,
        not his drug.
He should not have seen you
as his dependency;
he should have seen you as I do…
    … life-supporting."

He taught me what true love is:
helping each other breathe a little easier—
    smooth and steady—
instead of dying a little every day,
choking on being loved as someone's vice.

The *I'm Through* Haiku

I slept like a rock

Coming through my window

Woke up with a new light

The Mermaid and the Mariner

I took my headphones out into the breeze
and silenced the world while trying to remain in it.
I can no longer feel my own wind
because it is all lost on hot air
(at least, that's the way land dwellers see it),
but I'd love for you to have to sit here
out in this sunshine,
with nothing but rain falling
on your insides.

The storm is raging,
and all that I have in front of me
is the proof that that is okay.

So, today I am drowning out my eardrums,
drowning out my heart,
drowning out my lungs—
because I am underwater—
and I am looking for some light down here
in this abyss
where I can scream and no one has to listen.

Ink Blot in a Poet's Bloodstream

Forever the mermaid
who falls in love with the grounded mariner,
forgetting that she doesn't have legs,
because she only swims
far below the surface
where she can make things calm
and quiet
and peaceful.

Today she can't.
Today she's swallowing all the salt.
Today she's the only one in the sea
that's even half human.
Today she's all alone,
and all she has in front of her
is proof that that is okay—
just two swallows away from…
swimming with dolphins,
or being eaten alive by sharks.

As the drunken sailors try to hunt her down,
she flaps her tail as hard as she can
trying to find a cave—
ANY FUCKING THING—
that will make this ice cold water
not take her down in the undertow.

Heather Angelika Dooley

So, I will do the liberties;
I'll drown myself—
drinking like a fish,
forgetting that I am half human—
just to save everybody else.
Isn't that what the mariner has been telling me?
I think I have hit a break in the *current*.
I think this is where it carries us off to other hemispheres.
They'll all look the same underwater.
As we turn around looking for each other,
I already know that we're never going to find the other again.

The current's run is too wild,
and we created it.
A mermaid and mariner have so much romanticism,
but too different of backgrounds.
One breathes on grounded land,
and one breathes above and below—fluidly.
This is how she always gets stuck in their nets.

They both try for the sake of fascination,
but unlike the mermaid's lungs,

fascination runs dry.

So, they wave at the shoreline
and go back to being whoever they were:

half humans without each other.

Eventually, her scales always grow back.

You can't keep her grounded for too long.
She doesn't want planted feet.
She likes swimming the deep.
She likes the sunshine, her wind, and the dark abyss
that lives in her fins.

And, all that she can see today is…
proof that that is okay.

Heather Angelika Dooley

Everyone's One True Love

I'll only ask you once to hold my hand in this life.

Otherwise,
  I already know it does just fine
    holding my other one.

Laughter Should Always Be Reckless Abandonment

Little girls start changing their laugh as they get older.
Their rhythm changes…
Their stories, joys, tickles, and merriment do not change;
>>they do.
Their laughter becomes about chagrin, apology, and cordiality.
It becomes a nervous laughter.

It stops coming from a place of pure abandonment anymore;
it comes from a place of
abandoning their
>>pure abandonment.
They forget how to laugh from the bellies of their being.

All laughter is supervised by the brain.
(Oh, what a foe it becomes to the friend, over time,
when the two live side-by-side in the apartment of your head!)
It is sad when all of the stories, joys, tickles, and merriment
start to listen to generation, tutelage, and culture.
It is sad when laughter becomes about
>>acceptance.

Laughter should always be contagious.
It should never be about acceptance, apology, or cordiality.
Life is not a laugh track on a TV show
prompted by an audience's approval or final blow.
Laughter is about that rib-tickling, unable to breathe, authentic belly laughing
that comes from an unstoppable and unappeasable place.

Laughter is the universal human vocabulary.
You can say it all without saying anything but chuckling—
sniggering, giggling, guffawing, chortling, and tittering away—

without even thinking about anything unless it's funny.
There are no fancy words when something tickles your fancy.

Little girls:
You have to learn to ignore that dry roommate
in the apartment in your head.
Let them go to bed
while you stay up and party.

If I had any advice for little girls,
it would be to never grow up.

There is nothing more contagious than a child's laughter;
this is an infection that should always be infectious.
This is a condition that we should never try to cure.
There should be no such thing as nervous laughter.
We little girls have no place for that here
        where everything is short,
and pure abandonment should always be reckless and lifelong.

Don't change your laugh for anyone or anything, baby girl.

Abracadabra

Life goes by so quick
    when
each day goes by in
    slow motion.

My life feels like a 21st century movie
portraying that "person" whose life has become…
    desensitized,
    and has yet to realize
    the magic tricks.
I don't know what will arrive in my hat,
but I am definitely pulling up *hairs*.

I wear my seatbelt,
but I smoke cigarettes.
I do only what I please,
but I live with so many regrets.
I tell everyone that crying is bold,
but I'm all dried out.

It's been said that taking one day at a time
is what life is all about,
but I only go minute by minute.

Life is going on without me,
    even when I'm in it.

Heather Angelika Dooley

It's all a conundrum, isn't it—
forgetting the mixed tape in the car…
feeling forgotten when…
so many people are thinking of us?
Drinking when we should be eating…
sleeping when we should be making love…
thanking God above when we don't have enough?

Each day is a mad rush to something irrelevant.
We measure our pricelessness by our successes, which…
    still equals money.

Life goes by so quick when each day is a mad rush to slow motion.

We eat fast food so that we can go to bed on time,
    but, trust me, everyone wakes up too late.

Invaluable Lessons

We forget to thank those
   that hurt us the most.

Heather Angelika Dooley

Writer/Lover Confidentiality

A good writer
   never tells your secrets,
     they tell their own.

They sacrifice themselves
   and surrender you.

Spot Healing Tool

Once upon a time ago, you loved me in Photoshop.
I was an airbrushed version of myself in your eyes—
edited clean of imperfections and infections of the pneuma.

You had this amazing tool you used to see me through.
I was edited of all the blemishes on my record, and…
every small radius had your touch on it because I was

free of all the dust and scratches of all those eyelash
wishes that didn't come true. It was you who
perfected my pixels and forced my threshold to zero.

To you, I was a smooth blend of scars and defacements.
You un-blurred all the complexions that I found complex;
you filtered out the plastic and the fake of all my mistakes.

Once upon a time ago, you loved me in Photoshop.
When I was monochromatic, you gave me texture.
You went through my layer mask and hit……*Reveal All.*

I remember when you stared at me like I was saturated;
but, sometimes I don't remember that *once upon a time ago*
without seeing your background image losing its magic lens.

Heather Angelika Dooley

Prelude to an Open Door

When molecules dissolve in water,
they have a positive AND negative end.
This is called a solution.

When you come to a conclusion,
this is the conception of new connections
to make a good final impression that ends on a high note.

When a green anole lizard's tail breaks off,
this autotomy potentially saves them from a predator,
and then it regenerates and this is the emergence of a new tail.

When we read the epilogue,
it is the final chapter at the end of the story—
wrapping up the loose ends for the starting point of a future prologue.

(It is the same thing when you get to the denouement of any body of
    work…
matters are explained and resolved,
so we're free to move on to a new origination of ideas!)

When we make a resolution, we resolve something,
and though this is ultimately the culmination of something also,
it is usually a commencement of betterment and inner peace.

When there is a television finale,
this is the kickoff of a new show.

Ink Blot in a Poet's Bloodstream

When there is a termination of employment,
this is day one of a new path.
When you cross a finish line,
you step straight into the outset of some other accomplishment.
When an era comes to an end,
history turns into the dawn of another time.
When we climax,
ecstasy ends and this is the rise of dopamine.
When you call off a relationship,
this means you're free to start something again.
When love comes to an end in your heart,
it is open to the genesis of a new love to take root in its place.

So, what is the point of all of this un-poetic blather and bafflegab, you wonder?

Every ending is always a beginning.
Without endings, there would be no beginnings.
I don't know about you,
but you can't begin to live without knowing how to end
                                                                   well.

Heather Angelika Dooley

Final Eternal Sunshine

When you fall in love for the last time,
    it becomes the first.

We All Move Out and Move On

Sometimes I think of you
and realize there's always a part of you
that will be home to me.

After all those years,
there's a mortgage I can't deny that I paid.
But,
over a lot of time,
I've found a new home,
and it's the one we dreamed of
when we were kids.

This is the home that I store all the things I actually use.
This is the house that has the glasses and mugs—
the fine china, the holiday decorations—
the montages of photos on the wall.
This is the house with the pots and pans,
the shampoo and conditioner,
the tools and Christmas light strands.
This is the house with the marriage license,
the shared last name, the family, the future.

This is where I long to get home to after vacation.

This is where I feel comfy in my pajamas.

This is where, no matter where I go,
my bed is here and none is better than my own.

Heather Angelika Dooley

When I think about you,
you can never be him…
When once upon a time ago, I never thought there WAS
                        a him

that could ever be you.

You will always be a bit of home,
but in that way that I go to the house
where I grew up.
In a way I can remember that the office
was once my bedroom, and
my favorite mug will always be in the pantry—
because that's just the way it is.
In that way that you only go home so often
                                  because
your new home is your real home,
and the other one is just for childhood.

And past lives.

And what-once-was.

And once-upon-a-time-ago.
I let go so that I could.
It's still there,
and it's still real for space and time,
but now it's like a gingerbread house,
or your nursery school classroom…
You just revisit it to remind yourself
of who you once were

before you became who you were

always meant to be.
All my memories are now a vacation
that I might enjoy,
but can't ever wait to get home to my own bed
                                  anymore.

Deadbolt

If you're going to force me out,
> someone else will find their way in.

> That is key.

Frozen Food

My stomach is growling.
It isn't because I haven't eaten anything;
it is a gnawing hunger pain.

I am hungry for the music I no longer hear
because none of us crave the same song.

I am thirsty for the words that I can't say
when they are put in my mouth,
even if I refuse to swallow.

I have a vitamin deficiency in my intimacy
because passion has become a TV dinner—
quick and easy, single-serving.
There's no time for love when technology
is serving something
     more deserving.

I need more protein in my poetry.
I don't care if you cannot chew the fat of my words,
my stomach is growling
and it is because…

    I am starving.

Heather Angelika Dooley

Lilies

I was full of innocence—
of the way that love should
smell of lilies,
and feel heavenly like
velvet against freshly
bathed flushed flesh.
I woke up to moon filled skies
in daylight hours.
I was a model romantic
with chocolate kisses
for any unsweetened soul
who needed a little dessert in their lifes.
I opened wounds
and planted daisies.
That is when I dotted all of my i's
with pale, pink, tiny hearts:
when I still knew how to whisper
each and every word I said.

I giftwrapped the world
in star printed paper,
doing this with fingers crossed.

Ink Blot in a Poet's Bloodstream

I was full of innocence
      then—
of the way that love should
smell of lilies.

Heather Angelika Dooley

Unfair Taxi Fare

I've always kept one emotional suitcase packed.

With you,
I live out of one,

    every day,

and I keep a cab on speed dial.

Last Christmas' Poinsettias

Today I discovered that I don't have a green thumb
when I am wrapped up in last year's paper.
In fact, it is probably quite black—
but even négligée,
that a living thing can come back
in both torrent rainfall and blistering sunshine.

It just takes time and patience…
and most of all,
doggedness and resilience.

Parts of you can be dead and done;
but if your heart is won—
by the time it takes to stop and look around you—
you can overcome the most brutal of winters
if you keep the inner summer in 'splendant heat
right at your bare or bitter feet.

You get to decide.

Today that is my discovery, anyway.

Heather Angelika Dooley

There are always petals ready to open and mature,
and keep my limbs from being bare and splintered
in all I have to weather,
if I just wait for human nature
to take is course.

He's Charcoal Now

I couldn't brush my hair enough today,
twisted around petite knots
like fingers holding onto you.
    You made me;
    you ruined me;
    you threw me
    through the loop
    of all your entanglements.

He's charcoal now,
that's all—
that's not enough—
but, I had a say so,
and I said,
"Yeah, hop that bus."
I knew that I would be racing with my heart
    somehow,
going underground on a duck pond bench,
knowing I had lost him
    now;
and that I should have stopped long enough
    to see your glory.

He wore cotton hoodies
and smelled of designer cologne,
even though he grew up in a trailer
in some *Podunk* town with only one stoplight.

He said, "Whitey would pay",
but he was just a country boy,
and his mind was too convoluted, yet simple,
to put faith into the truisms of street clichés
that he knew so little about.

I wish that he had let me in.
I waited for the invite,
    but he was too shy
        to throw me a party
           in this big city.
It's because he started off
    too big for it.

His mind had patterns,
patterns that made puzzles,
and puzzles that became mazes.
Those mazes had color and became
    labyrinths—
labyrinths that went crazy like
    jungles—
and all he could trust me with
was letting my fingers get lost
    in his curls.
I played in there,
for years trapped in his hair
(that overthought and provoked lair)—
the only thing between my thoughts
    and his:
        the air.
But, he was smart
to not trust me enough.

Ink Blot in a Poet's Bloodstream

He knew.
The open air looked at him with slight eyes,
issued him binds of lies,
    like library cards
       …full of fiction.
And I knew this, so how could I forget?
Along the way,
I turned into every other female
    he ever loved.
    It was his destiny
that gave me the permission
to pull his hair again.

My "Muse"—
my same lame excuse.
God, I don't know where I was
when I turned to you,
just to return him, overdue.

He's charcoal now.
I waited for the invite,
    but he knew
that I was another library card
    full of fiction.

I used the same lame excuse
while lost in his curls.

Featherweight

I felt you so hard
        that you became, quite possibly,
            the softest plunge that I ever took.

You definitely K.O.-ed me
when I wasn't even looking (for)…

Only a sucker could be punched
and not feel suckered at all.

It might be true that I am a lightweight when it comes to
        falling in love,
             heavy.

Opalescent Beetle on Her Back

I panicked.

I thought,
'This might be the day
that I go from young to old.
This might be the day
that changes everything.
This might be the day
    that he
has to put my pants on for me;
I won't be able to make my own tea in the morning;
I'll cry out for mercy
underneath my cloudless smile
and waggish jokes;
I'll end up in bed—
    on my back—
because it feels too hard
to pick up my own slack.'

I panicked.

Could this be the day
that everything changed?
I sat up and the pain seared—
from my shoulder to my ring finger…
    …from ear to ear.
It hurt so bad that my eyes teared,
and my brain said to me,
"Go with it, my dear",
    and I cried
because my eyes had already started the job.
(Up until this point,

I have never cried for anything other than
happiness, loss, and empathy.)

Panicked and pained—
unable to take a deep breath—
I went out to the patio at 4 p.m.
and poured a glass of wine.
I had exhausted all in me that was exhausted,
so let's give this a try?

I sat there,
staring into a future of when young turns to old
without giving a fair warning
or asking my permission.
I sighed cavernous sighs,
put all kinds of pressure on the muscle (over)ruled,
and questioned how much more I could handle.
I felt my future loneliness sear.
From ear to ear,
my mind fretted that *old* was going to take the young out of me—
the wind out of my sails on an open sea—
just like my breath steered much too clear for me to want to see beyond a flat earth I never believed in.

While I sat out there in the fresh air
that I couldn't catch—
drinking a glass of wine at 4 p.m.,
and escaping the glass ceiling of life
that I did not feel that I could break today—
I heard an undersized rustling in the leaves behind me.
I turned around to see
an opalescent beetle on her back.
She had fallen off a wee stick and was struggling.
All of my pain and suffering eclipsed my mind,
and I got up to help her.
By the time I got to there,
she had flipped herself back over.

Ink Blot in a Poet's Bloodstream

I thought to myself…
'I am panicking.
I can get off my back,
roll over at any time—
and even if I am on my knees—
this is not the day.
I can cry in pain,
but I will always get up
for empathy.'

Sometimes our arms
are also legs.
We need to use them.

That opalescent beetle was on all fours
because she only knows walking
    is to crawl
        also.
Her hands are also her feet.

That is how you
shatter a glass ceiling
that takes the wind out of you.
You just get up again,
    out of empathy,
to flip the little girls and guys—
who are never as little,
    young,
        old,
or panicked and pained
as you thought—

    over—

Heather Angelika Dooley

if they cannot do it themselves.

Today I panicked and didn't think that I could,
    but I did.
Even when you're down,
your right side is…
    …up.

Opalescent where it is needed.

Mileage

Sometimes it is the distance between us

    that keeps us close.

Heather Angelika Dooley

A (Wo)Man of Sixty Winters

Somehow we're always stuck between autumn and spring—
just two feathered wings amid two bodies, trying to fly to
      another place, warmer, we have yet to find.
From your winter solstice, to my vernal equinox, we've met
      (somewhere/somewhat) halfway
    amidst the summer hemispheres. For years,
    I've just passed from one climate to another,
    torn asunder—living in nothing more than
    Januarys and Februarys and, of course, Decembers.

This bitterly cold weather is a shift from an even colder half of year.
It's as if we're back to some sort of embryonic development that
      brought us to where we started: an inertia of life—
      changing positions like atoms within a molecule—
      the cruel, cruel curse of the winter sunset…
      a reminder that natural light comes and goes
          as it damn well pleases.

Everything concealed in autumn is to be harvested in spring or early summer,
       but...
    the winter wry goes awry
    all of the time
        when
  we're used to resettling before we're planted.

  A (wo)man of sixty winters may never bloom in such an icy tomb.

Heather Angelika Dooley

Nobody Walkies the Talkies Anymore

Looking at the drones
staring at their phones,
I can't feel anything anymore.

I cannot reach anyone
unless it is through a radio transmitter,
looking for an electrical signal,
but always coming up short as
    the receiver.

This indispensable tool
has made me a dispensable
    tool.

While I sit on the back steps,
waiting for connection,
I realize I have no more connectivity.
My signal strength is clearly weak,
if my battery does not save lives,
and the tower that I try to be
puts me behind the bars
that keep us from talking to one another
when everyone is more concerned about how many they have.

    Close distance
    has become my long distance.

Ink Blot in a Poet's Bloodstream

Life has become:
video games and live streams,
reaching out to strangers to share dreams...
talking about important things
to open air and vacant, vapid memes...
posting things you want to be seen,
but knowing that a click of "Like" is all that it means...
sitting at dinner eating with family,
and feeling your thoughts are less important
than media newsfeed.

So, I ask you—
and answer honestly—
are you lonely?

We'll never know,
    will we?
Because that would not be
    post-worthy.

No one gets "Likes"
when your battery drains faster.

Slumberland

For those that say it is better to sleep when you're dead…

They mustn't dream like me,
for there's no sleep in my asleep;
my slumber's the liveliest place to ever be!

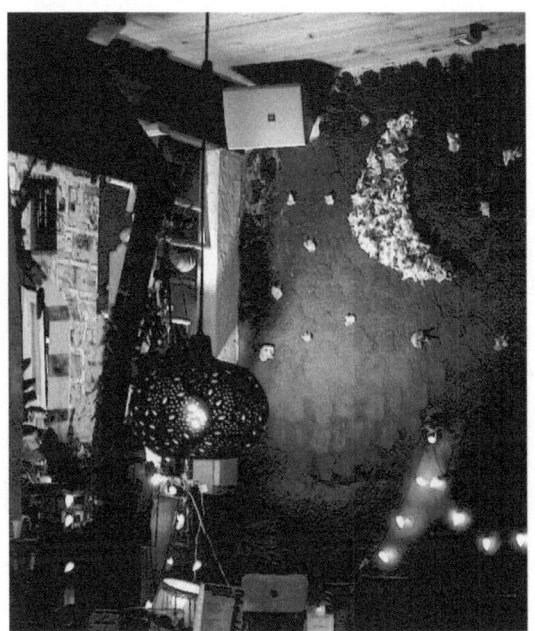

When a Bolt Bolts

I can't write anymore
if you won't let me read.

Lock and key:
that was never supposed to be about
    private diaries.

It is because it was never about
a lock and a key—
it was about a combination.

I will always remember the integer
that opened me up;
but it is clear to me
that you will always forget the
final unit,
because that's easier than finding out
what is left inside
when you can't *Master Lock* me.

Go ahead…
forget the combination.
I'm finally okay with admitting
that we were always at a
    deadlock
        anyway.

Heather Angelika Dooley

Joyride

I've been coasting down these open roads alone for so, so long—

traveling the roads less traveled on my own, taking in the scenery.

But, now I am here to s(t)ay…

you can ride in my sidecar, any day.

Ink Blot in a Poet's Bloodstream

These Germs Aren't for Pirates

You walked through my entry
and I could feel every fiber of your being,
    but your bounds held up all resistance.

Your eyes said it all, 'I want to, but I can't'—
underground defenses, above ground
              …and against.

Just the trace of your organic scent sends my senses into turbulence;
    my appetite becomes ravenous and my passion runs deep like
        jewels buried in the sand on the dark sea floor

long-forgotten precious fossils in the watery earth.
Even the abrade of your unshaven cheek sends me
    into a sleek kind of heat.

Every organ in my body suddenly has a rhythmic beat,
    and I can't love you in vain if these veins coarse you
through me,

      this hair-raising way that they do.

Your layered, sweater-y, thickset hug around me—I dared to dream of
your bare, balmy,
broken-down skin tangled in mine.

It was a twist of artless fate in my mind.

I watched you pull away…

    on your "Naked" bike.
      I was covered in a trench coat,

        but more than naked enough for the both of us,
        and I knew:

Wherever you go, there I will be.

    Because, even from my modest front porch,
      you're the deepest running vein in the floor of my dark,
bottomless sea.

The Gateway

When tongues lack bravery

    and hearts protect their own,

        eyes always tell the truth

Heather Angelika Dooley

Keeping It All Inside

Little snail,
out after a hard rain,
hiding in her shell—
trying to make it to the
    wishing well,
but being told
that she's too small to
lift the pennies in…
because she did not make them
    on her own.

Little snail
taking life at her own pace—
recognizing this isn't a race,
but everyone is standing
at some imaginary finish line
telling her she is always
    wasting
      their time.

Little snail
doing her best.
Little snail
who can't do enough for the rest.
Little snail
out on the steps…
she just wants what is best
(for everyone else),
but she'll never be at hers
with them keeping her
hidden (with)in.

Maybe this is why
little snails move so slow…
they're dragging their wishes,
everywhere they, apparently,
never seem to go,

    from inside of their shells.

I Love With Kerosene

Mother Teresa said,
"To keep a lamp burning
    we have to keep oil in it."

Now, I am no Mother Teresa, but…
I am not even dealing oil
because when you mix it with water,
    well,
        you know…

We all know:
I love with kerosene.

I'm a fuel.
I go beyond lamps.
I heat homes and I…
    …jet
    engines.

And, if I can't light your way after that,
other artificial light can guide your way,
    because
I'm tethering this Heather to a…
    moon
    to stare right into the sun.

Ink Blot in a Poet's Bloodstream

I assure you that I can't go blind
    staring
        straight into you.

Heather Angelika Dooley

In the Dark

It has taken me four days
to figure out where I stand,
    and it's not beside you.

He said that I fall in love
with *normal* boys—
something that I am not.

I went back to my roots
when you were away;
somewhere that I always try to fight…
    not to stay.

But, it's in the dark
that I belong.
It's in the dark
that I have always been…

    with things like you.

So many things in this life that **you** would
    consider trash
        are my personal diplomas,

Ink Blot in a Poet's Bloodstream

    my favored scars,
    my most priceless junkyard.

So many things that meant nothing to you
are the encyclopedias to my whole,
are the ticket fares to my soul,
are the things that I repoed
when I caught you dressed in black…
wearing the things you've stolen,
filling pockets of me,
    swollen.

It is always me who ends up paying
for trusting trusty thieves like you
who collect hearts in metal carts
and try to recycle them
while they are still full—
    open,
but not even close to empty—

me bailing them out for bailing on me.

It took me four days
to see where I stood,
    and it was never beside you;

you didn't give me enough room.
He said that I fall in love…
with *normal* boys—
something that I am not.
But, the trouble is,
you're the only one that thinks
that means trouble.
Isn't that the kettle calling the
bandit black?

It's in the dark
that I have always been

    with things like you.

Gut

Don't think twice;
once is enough.

If you have to think again,
it will always be a second thought.

Heather Angelika Dooley

Streetlamps

Wilhelmina is reading us books
that a thirteen-year-old would read
away at summer camp for the first time
(even though she is only six).

This front porch has always felt like summer camp—
its jerrybuilt swing and creaky wood planked floors.
I remember the first summer when we strung sprinklers
around the precipice like toy lanterns.

I hang my bare feet off of the frayed recliner
showing off my early May flip-flop tan.
It wasn't long ago—and it was so long ago—that I…
wrote about how I bit my nails down to the quick, right here.

This spot is the same spot that I always end up.
I always say that I won't come here again, but somehow I do.
Something about it feels like home. This is the first place
I came that day I drove into town. I remember being surprised

he had a spray of gray throughout his hair,
and he wore shark bone necklaces at the same time as
a shirt with the collar flipped up; he was a brainteaser,
and now I feel like the tease for adoring all of our differences.

So, here I am at summer camp, three years later,
and I still find this porch peaceful and an *uneasy breezy*;
but then he says, "How about you close your poetry
and try hanging out with us?", and I know the…

eventide music is over before it ever even dreams to begin.
No one can decide what to eat for dinner, what to do with
idle time, without this uneasy breezy girl making the rules.
As I wait for the moon, all I get are……streetlamps.

I can hear the moths cracking and burning on the bulb.
I see myself as one of them, flitting around this porch light.
I can imagine me bewitched by the wink and sparkle,
but I couldn't imagine myself taking up camp here, forever.

I am suddenly abundantly aware that this is not even summer yet.
This is just a porch with a jerrybuilt swing and creaky planked floors,
a frayed recliner, and splays of gray hairs just (now) taking root.
I remember that first summer when we strung sprinklers like toy lanterns…

Heather Angelika Dooley

Double Dutch

There's a place where my past stops
        and my future begins,
but if you don't jump in right on time,
        you'll never catch
        my
        rhythm.

Find yours simultaneous, quick-like,
because I am perfectly fine
        making a big jump—
        a leap of faith—
        without you.

Transient Heart Surfer

I am just going to keep
rearranging the furniture
so that I am always sitting
      in the light.

You can keep moving
your blowup mattress around
      in the night
where the shadows keep you pretty,
      and cover your face,
      so that no one can see
      that you have a home in me
      that you won't admit
      you'll never
          and always
            be:

the beach bum of my heart.

I'll follow the sun like a compass
and you'll lose your way,
      but for today,
you have a semi-permanent place to stay,
because, right now, you're not blocking my rays.

   Tomorrow?
Well, tomorrow is a new day,
and when the sun goes down,
    so do you.

So, start letting your hot air out now.
The waves are finally crashing against
    the rock
      you no longer have in me
        after high tide turns to—my—sunrise.

Rib Cage Cell

My mama said to me,
"You've always worn your heart
      on your sleeve."
(almost as if that was a bad thing),
      but that's not true.

I have always kept my heart prisoner
behind the bars of my rib cage
where it is in a 30" x 26" cell
while the rest of the world lives well,
      wild and free
to let their hearts weather against
the harsh conditions,
going numb to the cold,
and becoming indifferent
to the constant climate change
that happens with time and age.

My heart has never been that exposed;
      I have not let it be.
Every time my heart is up and ready for release,
I let it out into the world only briefly—
try to get it back into civilian life—
but it ends up right back in the pen,
because it is not true that I have ever let it
      wear on my sleeve…

…it's too damn good for that.

Heather Angelika Dooley

I don't want my heart to wear at all,
so I keep it behind bars
        where
it can live protected,
and in constant incarceration,
and rehabilitation,
so that it never becomes so free
that it forgets how to feel the things
that the wild and free have forgotten.

My incarcerated heart is never in the chains of freedom
to accept things the way that they are,
        as they are,
because hearts that have been wronged
will never be accepting of what is not right.

Ink Blot in a Poet's Bloodstream

Don't Knock It 'Til You Try It. Twice

It takes a lot for me to close a door,
   but when I do,

I slam it.

Heather Angelika Dooley

The Urn I Earned but Never Deserved

It won't be
   the fast food,
      the Nat Sherman,
         the Pinot gris,
            the cortisol,
               the cholesterol,
                  lack of exercise,
                     or sleepless nights of…
                          insomnia and nightmares
that kills me.

Let it be known…

it was the
     disappointments,
        abandonments,
           broken promises,
              lies,
                 deceit,
                    and abusers
that did.

Ink Blot in a Poet's Bloodstream

It was being called every nasty name in the book;
being told how horrible and *shitty* a person that I was—
a bitch, a bad human, the "C" word, and a loser of life—
yelling at me right in my face with a finger grazing my nose,
right after they told me how they loved me like no one else ever could.

That is what took me out.

I kept things together,
while I was—systematically—being pulled apart.

I wanted off that ride;
it was one hell of a roller coaster.
I once thought it was **my** pattern,
but I have learned it was broken people
not breaking patterns.

They all said,
"Just forget it! I didn't mean it, GEEZ!"
But that is not how this works.

I urn-ed this shit.

Heather Angelika Dooley

Keys to Life

He said,
"Everything you do is art…
from making a painting,
cooking a meal,
dancing in the living room,
drawing a picture,
mothering everyone around you,
writing a poem…
it is all a magical picture you color.
I am a creative person;
YOU are an artist!"

I told him,
"I am just going to keep loving
until my ink cartridge runs out."

Independence's Place

It has been nice
having your van in my driveway.
It reminded me of the visions I had
when I thought I was going to
have your van in my driveway every morning,
and your sleepy noises
the first thing that I heard in a day—
your tired head and peaceful face
what I would wake up to
in independence's place.

I'm sorry that we missed pouring coffee every morn,
and taking baths every Sunday evening
to catch up on each other's week.
I'm sorry that we missed picking out
the Christmas tree with the straightest trunk,
and all the times that my little random dances
would become annoying
(and, maybe, annoyingly cute).
I'm sorry that I never got to fold
your socks the wrong way,
and that something I can't find now,
    today,
got in our way.

Did you know?
(Oh, of course you didn't.
How could you?)
I've saved every fortune that I've ever gotten—
even when the cookie didn't make sense—
because all of those predictions are a part of
     our soon to be past *tense*.
From here, I'll save your pictures somewhere safer
than the albums they'll never make it into.
I'll save your shirt that you just thought you loaned me…
     The one I'll never fit in,
         again.
I'll save you when I lose a little bit of myself,
and especially when
I take that white dress off its shelf,
because you led me to believe
that you'd be the only one who would
     never
take it off of me so that we could hang it in the attic,
forever.

I don't think you ever knew
how I grew to…
Well, we'll just leave it at that
     now.

But, I will tell you how I saw where I could have gone,
and that's because I kept you free all along.
I never wanted to take you home
when you might not have found a home in me.
And it's ironic that all I wanted was to be alone
     before you;

and now, after you,
    I'm back at go
starting this game over without someone to play it with.

It's been nice
having your van in my driveway.
Maybe for just two weeks before you go,
I can have the vision come untrue, long enough to forget
when I thought I was going to have your van
in my driveway every morning,
and your sleepy noises
the first thing that I heard in a day,
as you whispered how you couldn't stay,
but "wished you could,"
in independence's place.

I told you,
"I never revise a poem.
Make sure, in your moment of self-defeat,
that you are sure,
because once I hit *save*,
    your decision will never

        delete."

Heather Angelika Dooley

Your Voodoo Doll Baby

I stopped telling you
   all of my secrets
when you became
   my biggest one.

Venus Verses Neptune

I feel like I have a planet in my stomach right now

from taking on the world.

My legs are like rubber bands;

my hands are trembling like my body's having an earthquake;

I feel leveled like a wrecking ball—

demeaned and disgusted,

heartsick and homesick—

for you…

the person I wish you were.

Today I hate myself for loving you,

and I hate myself for not being strong enough to love you

back…

Heather Angelika Dooley

when I know broken boys like you need me, too.

Today I hate this planet in my stomach,

and I hate the world I live in,

that now lives in me,

because I'm trying to swallow it

…all…

all because I love you more than the world,

and wonder if I should.

The Final Master*peace* Always Says Hers

Every artist suffers a little.
It's because they have
so much beauty in them
that doesn't always come out pretty.

It always comes out impressively unexpressed.

Their art hurts other people
because it shines so dull and dingy—
in the eyes of those who always want to shine—
that it takes the luster out of others,
    sometimes,
and it has so much truth in its hues
that it makes people want to lie…

    …to themselves in black and white.

That is never the intention of the artist.
The artist wants to paint the proper portrait.
The artist wants to illuminate the canvas or the page.
The problem is the truth is sometimes too bold.

The artist wants to put her heart and rage somewhere
    so that the art never suffers

    like she did.

Natural Disaster

June 19, 2005

Tornadoes are the most violent, forceful, and deadly

    natural disaster to touch land.

Just like her, they do their best to destroy everything in their path.

She hurls drama debris as far as she can spread it,

and the instant she sees you trying to rebuild,

    she strikes again.

Tornadoes devastate and leave a mess behind,

    just like your ending,

so the instant that *Psychlone* sees you rebuilding,

she's going to spin completely out of control, every time.

You can't get sucked into the same vortex twice

if you eject the monster from being it's own victim;

but until then, I'd pull in your rocking chairs,

lock down your trash cans and recycling bins,

and take your potted azaleas inside…

    …if I were you.

    Me?

I'm not hunkering down for anything.

I'm not chasing.

I'm just dancing in the rain.

I have spent years building an impenetrable fortress around my heart;

I'm not going to let a natural disaster like her level me.

    This is child's play

…for I am the eye of her storm,

and this ends up killing her, sadly enough.

The loudest siren screaming won't be as quiet as I am going to be

    in all my mon amour de soi.

They all ask,

"How do you put up with all of that crazy without losing your mind?!"

I reply, "I don't have to do a thing to provoke the tornado;

I can set it off just by being who I am."

That's the real force and power behind a strong wind.

Imprinted in 2010

I save a piece of paper that has

the indentation of your name on it—

    your signature…

    …move.

I knew that I shouldn't have let you

push down so hard.

    Your memory left a mark

    on so many pages after,

    if you couldn't tell,

    as I publish again

    to press on…

Phantom

In the few minutes that he sleeps,

I am with myself again—

that part of me that makes me…

   …me,

which is sometimes

   you.

Window of Opportunity

I've lost touch with myself.
It seems like she and I have not touched base for ages.
I can't remember the last time I talked to her, honest to God.
She's always been my best friend—my vicarious better half.
It's such a shame, really…
I wish I knew what she was up to these days.
        I really, REALLY do.

It's not as though you can close a bond like ours
when the room gets too messy; you can't just shut the door.
It's common knowledge they'll only open a window
        …and sneak out.
I don't know where she is now.
She could be on a train to the other coast, for all I know.
I quit listening to her wishes a long time ago.

Shame on me.

I was sitting on my back porch and my unfettered, feral cat
came up to the starting point of the stairs.
She wanted me to pet her.
She wanted to come inside for me to feed her,
but it had been so long since she had seen me,
she'd forgotten how to come home.
That is the same as it is with my best friend…*herself*…
It's been so long since she came home;
she barely recognizes me—or comme ci, anymore.
It's 'come clear that I have abandoned everything.

I saw my reflection in the dimmed out computer screen.
I had sacks under my eyes—I **miss** herself.
She's been so busy having her little girl's back,
that I have forgotten what it was like to see the other side of herself.

Shame on them for not listening to my needs.

I set myself free to the world. She would have been trapped here.
I wanted her to go off and follow her instincts.
Even if I miss her every day, I think of her constantly. I wish I could just call her and make sure that she's okay, but I know if she had my number, she'd call ME (out on it). I am the one who needs checking in on.

Heather Angelika Dooley

Foreclosed Heart

A poor choice
will leave you behind
    every time.

No matter how hard you hold on,
you'll end up beholden
    to the truth.

Don't keep coloring in their lines
waiting for them to sign on the dotted…
for you will become…
    …overdrawn.

Being honor-bound
often leaves you bound and gagged,
and while you're left hauntingly in arrears,
they'll be in the rearview—
    shedding no tears…
    for you…
all these years you suffered in their silence.

This is probably the only promise that they can keep—
the poor choice is always for keeps—
the debt is always greater than it seems.

Ink Blot in a Poet's Bloodstream

You'll be left behind,
because all the things you took into…
…when giving them the benefit (of the)…
    will become
      empty.

You'll be the one to pay
    your way
back into what they take into
    their accounts.

Dependents always become independent
because they know more than their adult children.
They learn to become their own child support.

Heather Angelika Dooley

That's Heaven

Every time you lie to me,

I still know your truth.

Every time you tell me

you're not allowed to love me anymore,

I can still hear the gospel behind your tongue.

And, that is not my silent desperation;

that is your desperate silence.

We've never been good at saying how we feel,

but we've been so damn good at speaking in tongues.

    So,

just shut the hell up and

    kiss me already.

Rough Draft

I have to know if you will read this

the same way that I wrote it.

I have to know how come

I can write thank you notes on the surface

of my coffee,

but not my face.

I can't make this piece of paper real.

I can't make my paintings come to life

where nothing has to have a definition,

but every fine line

is defined.

I have to know if you'll read this

the same way that I wrote it,

because if you can't,

then you're nothing more than a rough draft

that I don't care to edit.

There Is Only One Second Half

When the sun is behind you,
your shadow stands before you
catching light
    (weights)
        in your glove…
interpreting
    star
    players.

When the sun is in front of you,
your shadow is behind you—
    a strong specter shelter
    of semblance that is trailing secretly—
    not an absence of light form,
    but your inseparable companion.

But, when you step into darkness,
your overshadow faces you, and you are only
    a shadow of your former self.

Theoretical light is not enough to shed light on;
        everyone needs reflection.

Walk toward the sun
because no one has your back but
                      you.

Changing Reasons

Summer came before spring was even over.
I could smell Miss Ding's roses all the way
from my back porch farmer's chair.

I drank a half-gallon of icy green tea with honey
like it was just a Dixie cup of eau de cologne sweat.
Spiders rested on floating leaves as if they were

hammocks. Tomato plants rose from the ground
quicker than dough in an oven, and pollen
laced every seed and finger before it went down.

The spiking temps spiked a fever for cool commons,
so I made a plate of tapenade, bruschetta, and prosciutto
with orange creamsicle martinis flowing like a

Zen fountain. It was hard for me to believe
that I woke up that morning fighting back tears
for no reason and all kinds of reasons. It is still…

hard for me to believe that you have become no reason,
                                                           at all.

Heather Angelika Dooley

Manumit

Books are like lovers;
> you always love the latest
>> more than the previous,

but you always fear
> the latest
> is going to release
> too soon.

A Foreigner on Cloud Nine

In his faulty way of being American,
    he said,
"Making love to you made me floating."

His lenient poetry in an immigrant language
I have come to hear with the same ears
I needed to rear to unravel him,
like a hem in the gauchos that I wore last summer.

It's hard to believe that by my next release,
I will be leaving my thirties and heading into my—
oh, right now I can't even say it.

I wonder where he and I will be when I do

…release…

again—even if right now he says,
"I am on another planet in your arms."
But, right now, I am just trying to get this
paper airplane off of the ground.

I am trying to catch wind when he tells me that

I make his arms feel like cotton,

that these dark clouds have the look.

If nothing is heavy, than I don't know how to balance it.
So, if his arms feel like cotton and he says,
"I cannot lift them anymore…
    I am you;
      we are one",
how can I get these pages to float,
    or catch air,
      let alone land…
      somewhere?

Until then, I will unravel *hem*
and learn to understand the sounds
of an unsound American, rather it be
    him
        or
            me.

Plugged in Unplugged

Sometimes the loneliest place you will ever be
is in bed beside someone
you cannot reach.

There is no love
in our love

anymore.

Heather Angelika Dooley

Women in the Cabinet

He didn't see women as people;
he saw them as trophies,
and that is precisely why
                he never won me.

Stay-at-Homeless Mom

I don't want to leave here—
this place that I have always been.
But, I left, never to return,
yet, still have yet to leave.

I am stuck somewhere
that I am not even……there
                            anymore.

Meg had Mae three days before
I had my precious Mina.
Meg left her husband a month before
I left mine.
Meg met Frankie, and ten months later
they bought a house together.
Right now, they're shopping for
kitchen counters and cribs.
There's no baby yet, but they are already
making babies.

Meg was twenty when she had Mae.
She was twenty-three when she left her husband.
Meg is only twenty-five now.
She has her whole future and fortune ahead of her.

She's going back to her original plan.
She didn't have to leave this place for long.
She's stuck now, so she's not stuck
                    anymore.

I wonder why some things stick and some things don't…
Why does it work for some people and not other people?
Why do some people get to (be) stay-at-home when…
others have to leave?

I had it all BUT just one thing,
and I have finally let it soak in that I am sorrowed and angry.
How could he take that one thing away from me
…that he was never even able to give away?

His-story

Cleaning out history…
who needs all of this old junk, anyway?
I should donate it
to some other poor soul.
These love letters are wasted on me……now.

These words are useless.
More than words can say
can sometimes say *naught* a thing.
Actions speak louder than words…
when said at carefree(dom) breakneck speeds.

I should recycle all of this loose leaf and postage,
just like the sentiments have been repossessed
over and over and over again and again and again.
You weren't an original copy.
You were just a copy.

It's all been said before;
that doesn't make you a classic.
Your poetry is wasted ink.
Your heart is wasted muscle.
Your envelopes are wasted envelopments.

Heather Angelika Dooley

I saved too much
and trashed too little
while……you did the reverse.
If I didn't know any better, this was all rehearsed,
and your plan, all along, was to plan nothing at all.

I never signed (on).
I always delivered.
But, I definitely sealed
this coffin's deal shut……today
as I cleaned out his-story.

Don't write me anymore
because all I can do is wrong you.
My love is becoming a minimalist.
I have no room to store excess baggage,
so I am going to donate all your cheap knockoffs.

The Whole Package

People promise each other the world
until they are not given it.
We give until we no longer receive
something of equal or greater value.

Life and love is nothing more than

    re-gifting.

When we don't like what we get,
we save it for someone else,
and hope, with all of our hearts,
that the next package is better.

Dream Catcher

Gray days,
gray hair,
gray worries,
gray cares…
gray passions,
gray art,
gray love,
and gray parts.

I remember when all of my dreams were in rainbow.
Now, everything I do I have to Technicolor
because it's all become so black and white…
      so subtle hues,
no longer Prismacolor me and you.
I sharpen those pencils,
but they still come up dull.
I shade and shade and shade,
but it all comes up a shady review.

I miss the rainbow
when my dreams were caught
all throughout the day;
and not just late at night,
when I couldn't sleep
because everything was dark,
and too steep to climb,
and only in rhyme because
I have now become THAT gray poet.

And, what kills me the most
is that you know it,
but you have decided it is easier for my dreams
    to catch me
        than for you to.

It is all so much easier to live in that gray area
where you do not have to deal with my rainbow
    when it rains.
It is all so much easier to accept my gray,
and let me grow older instead of growing with you—
    us.

You'd rather me dream
than to live the dream.

    Because…

Gray days,
gray hair,
gray worries,
gray cares…
gray passions,
gray art,
gray love,
and gray parts
don't ask for anything

    from you.
They just leave it to sleep
in the daydream,

to catch themselves
in, what seems to be,
the fantasy and illusion
of Technicolor.

I have become someone that you want to watch
for a few minutes late at night—
a dead actress during the day,
trying to slay
a prism beam-splitter
of two consecutive frames of my single strip—
living in the gray area
of a black-and-white negative.

It's such a good thing that my dream catcher
      has never known such gray days.
The last thing that I need
      is your added film
         over everything.

I Was Taught to Slay Dragons

Mother's Day 2010

When I was a little girl,
I was taught to slay dragons.

I never cinched a corset—
I went straight into body armor.

I got clad with shield and sword
after Cheerios and a glass of OJ,

and before ever brushing my teeth.
I was taught never to wait…

for the white knight, but to…
saddle up that dark horse on my own

and (be)stride it all the way to the fairytale.
I never waited for a prince because…

I knew charm only went so far.

Heather Angelika Dooley

I knew early on that every prince

had a bit of ogre in them.
I learned to reside somewhere between

princess and wench—to always be…
a *fair* maiden. I was taught to conquer

kingdoms, and fight my way into the castle
without taking prisoners or…

becoming one of them. The riches
and power came from "Carpe Diem",

and that is how one seized magic.
I wasn't taught any of this by or through

books, and I didn't need a wizard to…
acquire skill. I was taught how to slay dragons

by my clairvoyant, my mere (im)mortal…
         Mom.

Teardrop Dance

We all know that nothing can grow
    if we don't water it.

So,
    sometimes,
    together,
we are going to have to
        drink up.
Throw away all abandon and run through the sprinklers,
and purposely forget our umbrella in the car.

Heather Angelika Dooley

A Logbook of Limbo

Time Heals All Swoons goes to the printer today.
I am already eighty pages into my next release, and
yet, I still don't know where it is going.

This might just be a logbook of limbo.
There is not rhyme or reason to my reasons or
my rhymes—I'm always and never out of time.

I don't want to work out in the rain.
I don't want to let the ice melt off of my heart, but…
it never fails that I do; I am too warm.

I'm so good at pretending to be light
that I've become nothing but dead weight.
Life can make you so sober that you can't even get drunk.

I hate days when there is no (long-)wind.
It is too still, too quiet, too hard to breathe.
My best takes so much effort, and it is still my worst.

I haven't always wanted to be this girl,
but I have no other choice than to be this woman.
I liked who I was, but I needed the chance at who I could become.

Ink Blot in a Poet's Bloodstream

Everyone has to work to live
when living is a job in itself.
I need to pay for this roof over my head,

but I haven't found shelter for my heart.
Time Heals All Swoons goes to the printer today,
yet, I still don't know where it's going…

Heather Angelika Dooley

Still and All

Am I the only person who just wishes you'd all sit still for a minute
                to capture something, like a mental snapshot?
I write my pipedreams out on paper so that they can stay *stationary*;
                    but, even my silent words aren't free from the noise.

Everyone needs to take their shoes off and just stay and sit for awhile—
hush your mind, free from turbulence, and listen to air.
                When nothing is flowing, everything flows.
                When nothing blows…
                life breezes in—
                effervescent like sweet Eiswein.

It might seem to be a motion picture, but at some point the feature stops.
Take that exposure and turn it into a charcoal drawing portraiture.
Hang your death above the mantle, now, for all it's worth,
                which is priceless.
Quit trying to get the lead out before it's been laid.

Every beauty has its beast, and it is only truly sad when all that shows up is
                the beauty.
Yet, what use is beauty when it's always been perfect?
Stop. Just stop for a minute.
Sit in the dross for awhile. See if you're even still here!
At a greater distance, we're still in the past or future, so please stay present.

Still and all,
when you come to me, all I want is your attentiveness.
I don't care about dazzle or overawe.
I do not care about grand plans and busy schedules.
   I care about
…sitting still for a minute—
taking your shoes off and staying for awhile.
I care that we have time to take a mental snapshot.
That is ALL that I have ever wanted from all of you.
I don't need the charcoal portrait over the mantle later on.

You can't chug or guzzle a sweet Eiswein.

Table d'hôte

We don't have a choice of whom we fall in love with.

We don't have a choice of whom we fall out of love with.

We only have a choice to stay or leave—

    it's a set menu at a fixed price.

But, what if we don't like either of our options?

I Forgot My Keys and Locked Myself Out of Me

My body has quit generating its own warmth.
The heat of a 450 degrees oven warms me now.
I bite my nails down to the quick and think,
'Well, damn, that was quick. Now what?'
Yet, I have the heat of a fever burning inside of me—
    sometimes down to the crisp.
I expand
and evaporate
at the same time
because
damn it, I am so fucking out of the time I am wasting
on this doorstep of everything—and nothing—waiting to get in!

This non-mechanical transfer has transferred me to…
    you…
    whoever you are.
    I haven't found out yet.
This hot season has to come with searing spices
because I need more flavor and less fluff.

The heat of passion is not always enough.

In the heat of my desires, I forgot the keys and…

    …locked myself out of me.
I finished us in one carnivorous bite, before and after,
I never finished what I jumped on board to do.
That was to melt metals, inflame me, and to find the
    keys to *home*.

But, this burning sensation is not electric energy…
It is simply the heat of battle.
A heat not fit to cut and (re)move my bolt(s).

I forgot my key.
The question is:
who do I call now?

Landlords and locksmiths have become more loyal
    than you
when you're the only other person that I gave a copy to
    in these places that I can only seem to rent.

A Vow Forever New

For as long as I shall live,

I look forward to never growing old

                with you.

Heather Angelika Dooley

Sleep Tight on Your Right Side of the Bed

There was once this little girl,
    who was actually a woman,
who had a little girl of her own.
She fell in love with a man
    who was actually just a
    little boy.

The word familiar and family are so close,
but you're so far away from knowing what that means
    when you harangue about intimacy.
Intimacy is an affectionate relationship with
    a person or a…
    group,
and I am, and always will be, a group from here on out.
I was a couple before you and I ever became…
    …one.

Last night she and I fell asleep on the couch.
You woke us in that time between night and morning.
I scooped her up like a sandbag and carried her to bed—
    MY bed.
I settled her down under the covers—me the meat in-between—
and you said, "Babe, why would you put her in your bed?
That's not normal. I guess this means there's no more intimacy
    for me."
    Ah, yes, for "me"—his favorite word.

Ink Blot in a Poet's Bloodstream

He lulled for a moment and said, "That is not right."
I replied, "She has more of a right to be here than you."

We do not live together.
    We are not engaged.
        We are not married.
And every day, I become more painstakingly aware that...
    we are not family.

So, don't sit preaching about intimacy from your ivory tower
    when all you're prying for is privacy.
    You should feel lucky to have four arms around you
    instead of just two. You should be honored to wrap
    yourself around two bodies, instead of feeling up just one.
It isn't all of the time, so for one night you could shut up and see
when you got me, you got a group—a couple—and you got more
than most people could ask for. But, you're accustomed to asking
for everything when you're only allowed to have what we offer.

At first light, you asked me to take her to her own bed again.
    Again, I said, "No."

    When you become a man,
maybe you'll be able to sleep beside a little girl.
    Until then, have fun
sleeping on your *right* side of the bed.

Heather Angelika Dooley

You Can't Make Memories in Messenger

We oftentimes sit around lamenting about how we need

   a best friend;

but oftentimes, we just need a friend,

   at best.

Palette Clean

I have you memorized
the way that I can start humming the next tune
to a soundtrack before it ever comes on…
    cue.

Today's another waste of makeup.
Today's another day of looking pretty,
outside of your mirrored expression
looking back at my reflection.
I don't see the need
for all of this concealer
    over my
    tough
    skins.

I bronzed the flushed cheeks you missed.
I glossed over the lips you kissed.
I highlighted those bones you shadowed.
I put mascara on the bottom lashes of my eyes
because I knew you couldn't make me cry
    anymore.

I had you memorized
in that way that I can start humming the next tune
to the soundtrack of my life
    into play.

Heather Angelika Dooley

I wipe the
....
away
with my full foundation,
which is now just my bare and naked face
in the place of all that I concealed when we
    never found a song that rosy-d my cheeks.

Simplicity Is Best

Don't wait to be kissed—
    kiss.
Don't wait for your hand to be held—
    grab it.
Don't lay with your back turned
hoping they'll wrap their arms around you—
    roll over.

Don't wait to be loved back;
be the one to love first.

It never hurts anyone
    to keep it simple.

Heather Angelika Dooley

Loose Ends

You said you couldn't go
until you tied up some loose ends,
but you still haven't tried
to tie me up yet.

It's hot in this house,
while my head is in the air.
I don't want to convince you
that I could have stopped
your anger at your music,
but maybe you could have
thrown those punches with me—
maybe together we could
      kill the relief.

I bought pictures of you
that I never knew.
I bought sizes I had never seen.
I bought all the things
I thought I'd come home to
in my famous back bend,
while you merely thought of me…
      as loose ends.

Ink Blot in a Poet's Bloodstream

It was so far away
on the other side of this page,
showering in a vacation
as you bathed in the rage.

I know what it's like
to have a red light caged in
      by your ribs.
I know what it's like to have
a bomb in your heart with a mouth
screaming before it kills you to get out.
I know what it's like to feel like
you have no control over the things that you want,
because like your drums,
I have my hands—
the two things I don't quite understand…
    …my paints
    and their restraints, and
    these binded lonely nights
    going to the press
    that pressed me between
a wall and pointed grinded down teeth in the sheets—
    because like your drums,
    I have you…
something I want to play every day
when I haven't quite found the way;
something I want to make a part of my life,
and yet, I've never looked like anyone's
    wife—
not on sheet music, anyway.

Heather Angelika Dooley

So, this is how I see it:
You said you couldn't go
until you tied up some loose ends,
but you still can't seem to
      tie me up
      yet.

Divided in Two

I took a sip from my mug
with a springtime light shower
washing my raw, ghostly skin.

I saw her staring back at me,
and we sat there for a long moment,
    holding…
…a silent conversation.

She said, "Quit trying to do it all.
If you keep trying to do so much,
everyone will never get enough."

I realized that if my cup is empty enough
to constantly keep meeting this stranger
at the bottom—
well, nothing will ever be(,) full(y)
    me
        when I pour too much.

Heather Angelika Dooley

Robotic Thrombotic

I'm waiting for my dam to break—
this stumbling block blockade that
obstructs the flow of my feeling water.
I'm confused, clogged, and choked by
all I can't let stream from my stream.

That inkblot in a poet's bloodstream…
lumps up in my mass(iveness)…
my blood pressure spikes while my
passion and desire coagulates and I
become (writer's) blocked and obscured from
those waterworks that are now just whispers.
This bard holds no bard on the page,
while her face holds no resemblance.

I'm an inkblot in a poet's bloodstream,
      that's all.

I'm just blood flowing through this
(full) circulatory system—all that's left of me…
the flow of the sheets of this bound (and gagged)
      living body.

Ink Blot in a Poet's Bloodstream

It's not as fatal as it sounds, really…
I put my plasma and platelets into pages
and my vitally principled red blood cells
into the cell of a cover I shed blood and sweat for,
but never tears. Like I said, I am waiting for the dam
to break this inkblot in a poet's bloodstream, then…
I won't publish the obstruction of passage…
    …anymore.

As long as these words, clear as mud, course through my veins,
the buildup won't take out the pump that pumps them out onto paper,
and the lack of tears won't take me out of this life where my deepest vein
    can't live

    in vain.

Beach Winters

After twenty-one years,
we met up again, so casually.
He said, "You look exactly the same,
but there's a sadness in your eyes now."

That broke my heart, but it was true.

For the next few years,
we played in beach winters.
We would go out together and people would say,
"Does your husband want another drink?"
I would reply, "He is not my husband."
They would respond, "Well, your boyfriend, then?"
I would answer, "He is not my boyfriend, either."
They would look at me—fuddled—and say, curiously,
"Honey, there is no way that's true; not with the way that he looks at you!
I have been a bartender for years and I know when a man loves a women.
That man only has eyes for you."

Four years later, I could have thrown my arm out and touched a life raft.
We ordered clams and mussels. The waitress asked if I wanted lemon with my water.
I felt his hand on my knee. I reached down to clutch it. He held it still—too still.
He slowly slipped something on my finger. I froze. He made that face…
the one the bartender mentioned:

only eyes for me.

He said, "I don't want there to be sadness in your eyes anymore."

The waitresses waited for to me react. They were in on this.
I pulled my hand back and stared at that dazzle and flash.

Not the ring. Him.

I could have thrown my arm out and touched a life raft, right then.
I had. He was. I knew it then. I know it now. I just wasn't ready,

but I said I was, looking at the flashy dazzle in his eyes for me.

I said yes for 36 hours. For 36 hours I had someone who didn't want my eyes to be sad anymore. For 36 hours I could have thrown my arm out and touched a life raft. Forever.

36 hours later, we went and got lotto tickets before going to his place to watch a movie.

He said, "Whatever we win…"

I had my legs wrapped in his like a two strand plated dough,
my head nestled on his shoulder, my own shoulder in his strangely comfortable armpit,
his arm draped over my chest as if a Boy Scout sash, so full of badges,
and I said, "We need to talk…"

Now, there was *a sadness* in his eyes.

I don't want to talk about that conversation. It was a moment that I held my arm out and let go of the life raft. I was a drowning idiot.
We scratched the lotto ticket and it was just two dollars.

He said, "We'll split it." He was being cute in order to make light of the fact that I ended what we could have shared.

If I had a dollar for every time that I regretted splitting that two…

I'd not have to remember, now, how no one has looked at me the same, ever since—

how I was only arms length away from a life raft, and I chose to tread water back to winters.

Just winters.

Why can't I ever see with only the eyes for me?

It's because I knew he deserved the same thing.

That breaks my heart, but it is true.

Rendered Speechless

Words are only words until there are no more words.
   Then, silence has enough sayings to make every book empty,
      every adage an adversary,
         and every psalm a swan song.

At some point, we just have to stop quoting
   and listen to the quieten that can't quit
      when we're afraid being speechless means…
         there's nothing left to say.

Killing Time

This abominable music is almost as

beyond the pale as their toilet water

sweat on the raggedy-ass, saw-toothed

towels. The halogen burn smoldering

my protégé pupils—eyes and nose and

ears hemorrhaging. The void plastic

voids caroming on the table, *rat a-tat tat*.

Killing time until I can dim the cry of high

notes. The tumult of metal fitting into metal,

the fortissimo force of close, un-melodic. A

maddening beep of transactions. Promotions

wailing, televisions squawking, blenders

Ink Blot in a Poet's Bloodstream

bellowing—I am biting my brim as I hear them

bouncing the rim. Rubber against high-shine…

I'm just killing time until I can trade this fusty

fake air in for fresh. Monochrome conversations

and limbering limerick. Babes dressed for a barbell

bordello. I'm just killing time until I can feel the

puff of air on my knees and breathe deep with

five-finger exercises against the keys. Killing

time isn't going to kill me from what is gratis.

Heather Angelika Dooley

Penitentiary Perfection

Just pick up as you go
so that your life does not get out of control.

For four decades, I chased perfection.
I was taught that through observation,
but it is a place of detention
that does not keep you contained;
it has an open cell—
a house of *over* correction—
that makes you unwell,
and puts you out into a free world
that isn't free at all.

We are all just one person
sitting around waiting for what other people expect of us,
and expecting too much of ourselves
    when
we know that we can't expect anything
from anyone else but ourselves,
    in the end,
slammed in by the slammers.

So, just pick up as you go.
Pick up after yourself.
Do what you can when you can.
This isn't a life of perfection;
    it's a life—
a Big House that should be lived in.

Ink Blot in a Poet's Bloodstream

Let the toys decorate the house.
Let the coffee rings soak into the table.
Let the dust settle, at least for a little while
    (or for once).
Let the shoes on the couch,
the puzzles miss some pieces…
Let the pictures hang a little crooked;
let the holiday decorations stay up
    a little longer than needed.
Don't make it another young offender institution.

It's an okay stockade for today.

No one has ever died from eating cereal for dinner,
    or leftovers for breakfast.
No one has ever died from you not showering
    for two days.
No one has ever died from you not having a smile
    on your face.
No one has ever died from you listening to music in your headphones,
and ignoring them to write your poetry.
No one has ever died from you taking a break from all of it
to dance on the living room carpet in circles
for only as far as your headphone chords could take you.

You should never feel guarded in your guardhouse.

A lot of people HAVE died from expectations.
A lot of people have tried dying to meet them.
A lot of people have died trying to do everything for everyone,
living for everyone else's needs, wants, and feelings
    in their own *chokey*.

Heather Angelika Dooley

Just pick up as you go,
so that your life doesn't get out of control.

This includes your own stuff.
Pick it up…
    Your passions,
    your corrections,
    your artistry,
    your confinement,
    your heart,
    your stir,
    your needs,
    and most off all…
your convictions, prior and present.

Pick them up
so that you can go long and hard.
Don't cut yourself short
because others think you fall it, weak.

They don't know what it takes for you to…
be everything that you are,

    and that's the problem
    with expectation and perfection…
    neither ever feel lived in
    in a place where they are not
    dying to get out,

while trying to straighten up a messy life.

Sanctity

He said, "You must be beating them off with a stick!"

But, I think it is the other way around—

their sticks are beating me to a punch-line

that I've never been able to come up with

before they get inside that spot in my freedom of interference

that can be interfered by…

   aversion.

No matter how many tricks that this old dog learns

with sticks and stones,

I still go for the bone,

   every time.

Even Fireflies Fade Out Sometimes

Today I decided to do something for me,
and that is that I am doing nothing for you.

This is not a hostile move
    or punishment.
      It's my reward.
It's my reward for always feeling sullen
because I bring it on myself.
I worry every day I'm not enough for everyone,
and that's what's making me incomplete.

I can't see my light in the day,
even if it is flickering in some way.

Today my infrared and ultraviolet
are on a completely different wavelength.

I realize that no one is going to die
if I take this day to wallow in my writing,
    unless it's me.
Either way, when I don't pass (it) on,
    parts of me fade out.

Neil Young said,
"It's better to burn out than to fade away."
Even with a name like "Young",
he knew what it felt like to get old.

Ink Blot in a Poet's Bloodstream

The way that he and I see it,
the main source of light on this *Mother* Earth
> is simply not the sun today
> (or any day, I guess);
> it's the moon of our moods.

I've been fading out for a long time,
and even though I never begrudge it,
I know that I am dying away.

Life is good here,
even when I am not my best.
The trouble is, I don't know if
anyone else knows that.

I'm not sure that I am releasing energy,
to the living things in my life
that are supposed to digest them,
because all I ever hear is how empty
I make them feel with my fullness.

I don't know if I am releasing energy
into my lifework anymore—
to the nonliving things in my heart
that I always wanted to ingest it.

Heather Angelika Dooley

I'm always trying to be better
than so many people's worst,
and feeling like I am invisible
no matter if I fail or succeed.
    It would seem,
I've lost my bioluminescence;
the thing I thought that…
anyone who loved me could never stop
    seeing
because of how naked my eye has always been—
of how much I burn for them
so that they never fade away.

So, really… What's it mean to me
if I am always holding on for dear life?
Because a part of mine that I need,
I give away in this corner of myself
    in a Word document
    that no one ever reads?

Does that mean that I am dying or fading?

My constants in nature,
have become speed and intensity
… in a vacuum.

Ink Blot in a Poet's Bloodstream

Today is just one day that I need to
shed some life from my dark room
that has no room for anyone else
      in it.

Just for today, I am fading so that I don't die.

I'm just going to take my time
being a firefly under the moon of my mood.
I hope that you can all understand…

We don't always need to be on the same
wavelength.

Neil taught me that
when he was young.

I'm the girl who collects lyrics in jars—
not without puncturing holes in the lid
    so that they can breathe—
    because I don't like to smother
    living things.

Heather Angelika Dooley

Sometimes,
    fire
        just
            has
                to
                    fly.

Insufficient Postage

When you call and hang up
without saying, "I love you"

it's like writing a love letter
      and never sending it.

Heather Angelika Dooley

Your Largest Organ

I am such a free spirit

that

I sometimes feel claustrophobic

in

my own skin.

It's Funny Who Chimes In

On my wedding day,

I only got two text messages.

One was from my first husband,

and one was from my first love.

They both said almost the exact same thing:

"Happy wedding day. I am wishing you the best.

You deserve it. You deserve all of the happiness

that you give out."

I am paraphrasing, of course, but…

Oh, the irony!

The irony is that no one really knows the proper definition of irony.

It's actually:

"a state of affairs or an event that seems deliberately contrary to what one expects and is often amusing as a result."

Heather Angelika Dooley

But in this case, it was a little of both definitions.

Mostly, I know that those were the only two people to text me the day that I got married,

and it doesn't define me at all,

and does all at the same time.

My life is always ironic,

but I am lucky to have been loved,

however way, anyway

Cleaning Out Underneath the Couch

So many things fall out of our pockets

without us even noticing,

leaving traces of us behind.

We don't even know what they find

of ours

when we're long gone.

That's sometimes all there ever was,

and we need to realize that…

all they had to give

was something that fell out of them,

so long forgotten,

amidst the crumbs, worthless pennies,

and *lent*…

that didn't deserve your dent in the cushions

because you did not stay long enough

to leave an impression,

knowing crumbs and *lent* were all you were going to get,

and that was good enough for tonight.

Whatever you find,

I don't want it back.

That's why I came over here to begin with.

I'm not looking to clean up anything.

I've Learned Nothing is Really Waterproof

Here it comes…

that monster conversation

we've been needing to have.

I'll wear waterproof mascara today.

No, you know…

I won't wear any.

I'm sure today will be…

another waste of make-up,

for there's no

kissing and *making up* this time.

I've had my fill of wasting good war paint on you

for breakups that didn't deserve any of the glossed over words

that came from my sweetened, lyrical, high shine bullet lips.

I'm not going to wear anything

Heather Angelika Dooley

because I have nothing inside of me

to wash off, hide or protect anymore.

Dropping the matte finish

…for ours.

Let's Just Pretend

What you don't press
                is never forced.
What you don't push
                never needs to be pulled.
What you don't try to keep
                will never be lost.
What you don't hide
                will never be taken.
What you don't try to correct
                will never be mistaken.
What you don't hold onto
                will never need caged.
What you don't rush
                will never hurry past.
What you do not analyze
                will never need revealed.
What you let be
                might just...
                be.

What you don't invent
                might not pretend.

    (Let's just pretend we're all wild and free.)

Heather Angelika Dooley

No Better Half

I've discovered how close
    love is
      to hate.

I only love you halfway now,
and I love myself wholly,
therefore I know, at least,
    some part of us
      will survive this.

"Tom"

He was the kind of guy who opened the door for you.
He was the kind of guy who walked you to your car
so that you were safe, without any preconceived notions.
He was the kind of guy who pulled out your chair
        when you came in a room.
Hell, he was the kind of guy who stood up
the minute you walked through the door.
He wasn't trying to woo you; he was just that kind of guy.

You see… He had a girl. Her name was Laura.
He met her when he was only 21.
They had gone to school together in New England—
        he the artist, her a musician.
It was a love affair that all movies, books, and plays are made of.
He taught art classes and she played in symphonies.
He came home and drew her as she pounded on her piano keys,
and he could not have found another muse
that brought his fingers more life
like hers played away his charcoal and lead dreams.

Twenty plus years of tunnel vision,
        between art and love…
How we could all hope to have that many decades
        of a welcomed caved-in heart!

I met him modeling for an art class.
He saved me from some creep who
was waiting for me in the parking lot.

"Hello, I enjoyed our class tonight.
Why don't you sit here on this bench and look through my portfolio?"
"I really need to get to my other job."
"Okay, well, I was trying to be casual,
but this guy is waiting for you by his car smoking a cigarette.
Please, sit here and pretend to be interested in my work.
    I am keeping you safe."

That is how it started.
It started out in a parking lot with him having an eye on me.

Weeks later, I went to the local Irish pub
with a couple of friends to hear a band play.
I went up to the bar to get another cider.
I ordered and the bartender said, "It's paid for."

    There he was, right beside me.

I ended up never leaving that stool.
I stayed and talked to him until the wee hours of the night.

Over time, he and I became friends.
We were an unlikely pair—the Goth deejay and the Scottish painter.
I was at a place where I just liked his conversation.
It was so nice to have someone actually listen to me
    and care about the words I said.
I guess it was the same for him, too.
Here I was, surrounded by so many people
and without anyone. There he was without anyone,
but sitting beside me and thinking that I was enough people for him.
I'll never know what happened, how it happened, or when it happened,
but I kept finding myself going to where I knew he was.

Ink Blot in a Poet's Bloodstream

Outside of the pub stool, we had a love for
theater, poetry, books, art, music, and a damn good bourbon.
I invited him to go see an independent film with me.
I told him to meet me at the Hippodrome.
When I got there, he was standing on the stairs dressed in a suit and tie.
(*Boys* my age never did that.)
      He was so dashing.
I felt something in me flip over like a record.
I had actually never seen him that way,
but my needle skipped a beat.
There was a jump from my stomach to my throat.
      WHAT THE HELL?!
He was so handsome standing there, sideways smiling.
Never will I not be able to picture that mental Polaroid...

When the film was over, I asked him to go for coffee at Maude's Cafe.
We sat for hours and talked about everything
from Chaucer to Chopin to crappy migraines.
From there, I asked him to go for Sangria at Emilano's.
Again, we talked for hours about
      Klimpt, karma, and kismet.
Because he was the kind of guy to open doors,
      he opened my car door for me.
I leaned in to hug him, and then I put my lips on the side of his.
      He froze, stunned.
      I apologized.
He just stood there with his eyes closed, but he did not move.
I asked, "I'm going to do that again, if that is okay?"
He gently nodded, but rested his hand on the small of my back,
which felt like an invitation, and I felt his lips for the first time,

THIS time.
He held his eyes closed for so long, and I knew then…
…it had been so long.

I asked, "Would it be okay if we hung out more?"
He said, "I think so. Do you want to meet me at the pub?"
I replied, "No. I would like to meet you at your house?"

The house was full of Laura—
her baby grand, her sheet music,
photos of her on the built-in bookcase with her many instruments.
I had never had more respect for a man that I felt so sorry for.
It had been 7 years; he was still circling around her ghost songs.
    She was still so alive in him.
(Her garden clogs were even in the office, where she always left them.)

    I asked, "How about you draw me?"
    This was how it all began again.

For the next few months, we had a lot of paper, a lot of pencil,
a lot of moonlight in his sunroom, a lot of deep talks,
a lot of love with charcoal fingerprints.

We both knew that this was an unlikely pair.
But, in spite of all of our differences, he was what I needed.
I don't have to hope that I was what he needed—
I knew I was;
it was all over his sketchpads, face, and loosely tight holds to my lower back.
It was so damn organic.

Ink Blot in a Poet's Bloodstream

He read me poems from Yeats and Shakespeare,
and we talked about Vonnegut at lengths.
He drew me in still life ways I don't believe
that anyone has ever seen me before, moving.

    Charcoal. Dust. Everywhere.

He woke up before I did
and made me perfectly poached eggs, bacon,
and freshly squeezed orange juice,
bought me robes and new toothbrushes,
and pulled me down on his lap while I took my first sips of coffee
with contemporary symphony artists
that sounded like rock-n-roll gods pumping through the kitchen.
He was a distinguished man.
I was just a girl, but he never saw me as that.
I don't know what it was with us, but we made so much sense.
There weren't words for what we had.
We were what each other needed.
Maybe what each other craved?
All I know is that the whole world disappeared when we were together;
it was like the outside world went away
outside of the doors that he held open for me once I got in his *home*.
He said, "It took me 7 years to sit here with you.
I don't think it would make sense to most people,
but I know that Laura would love you—
      herself and for me.
      She would get us.
I don't think that there is anyone else who would understand that, though."

But, it did not make sense, not in real time.
One day, he met me after work, accidently.
He was going to his car and saw me standing outside the club that I managed.
I was SO HAPPY to see him.
I told him that I had to go home to feed my cat,
so I brought him home with me instead.
      Maybe it was a mistake.
      Maybe it was meant to be.
He went into my bedroom and saw my room
full of Hello Kitty stuffed animals
and a young girl's college futon,
pink and black everywhere.
He stopped and closed his eyes.
Even with his eyes closed,
I could see the pain in them.

He said, "What the hell am I doing, Heather?
This all makes sense at my house,
      but oh my GOD…
You're still a young woman.
      And you SHOULD BE.
It just hit me right where it hurts;
no matter how old your soul,
this just proved to me all of the life that you have ahead of you
      that I don't.
I can't keep doing this with you and feel good about either of us.
It's not right for me and it's not fair to you.
Or, actually, it's the other way around. I don't know.
I just know that I have to do the right thing right now."
We both sunk down on my college kid futon and cried.

That was the last time that he read me Yeats, Shakespeare,
or made me perfectly poached eggs over talks of Vonnegut at length
with his gently strong hand on the small of my back.

Eventually, I ended up in another relationship,
but it was all so complicated.
I can remember leaving a coffeehouse
where my new *boy* and I were basically "taking a break"
and I turned the corner, after that elementary conversation,
and there HE was, walking up the sidewalk.
We both stopped dead in our tracks.
He knew me so well, so he knew I was hurting.
We said not one word. He just grabbed me.
I shoved my face into his chest.
Again, he put his hand on the small of my back
	—his spot—
and his other hand on the back of my head.
We stayed that way for so long.
I took him in. So hard. It had been too long.
I pulled my head back and looked at him.
Just like that first kiss by my car, he closed his eyes and nodded.
When he opened his eyes and looked at me, he said,

"I fell in love with you, Heather. I fell so in love with you."

I said back, "I know.
We can't be what we're not,
so we have to love each other no matter what,
and it's just this. It's just always going to be this."

That was the last time I saw him.
That was the last thing I said to him.
That was the last time he pressed his hand on the small of my back.

Heather Angelika Dooley

Last year, I saw a post on Facebook…
The Irish pub patron "Tom"—
because of his uncanny, strikingly spittin' resemblance to Tom Selleck—
had passed from kidney cancer.
The exact damn thing that took Laura.

    …Soul mates until the end.

I choked and went to the porch.
I made a cup of tea and recited *A Drinking Song* to the moonlight.

I never told anyone about us because of our vast differences,
but thanks for always holding the door open for me, and holding me.
I hope you're proud of me now. I'm doing my best.
You were right, but I am so very glad that we were wrong for a little while.

    (P.S. – I still pas de bourrée to punk music, so…
    No, I still haven't changed, like I promised.)

Ink Blot in a Poet's Bloodstream

Love Is Blind

She asked, "What were Daddy's fingernails like?
I don't remember."

I wondered how anyone could forget such a thing,
for I could never forget a hand I've held.

Some people are *eye people*, *smile people*,
physique people, and even *butt people*...

I am a hand person. I notice everyone's hands, first.

When it comes to such a thing,
I have a photographic memory,
even though I study and read them...

in braille.

Now I'm a Blond

The sky got dark,
but never opened up.
    I knew
    that was you
    in all your symbolism.

I am not part brunette version
    anymore.

The first steps,
bright as diamonds
only your eyes had to offer…
I wasn't into material things then,
but my eyes were cerulean like the sky
    and yours…
    as richly brown as
            dirt.

I still get you stuck underneath the nail sometimes.

But, in all other aspects of life,
you were only the breath in my rhyming couplets—
poetry was always yours,
and since I have touched him,
I haven't had the time…
to put my hands on a pen.

Ink Blot in a Poet's Bloodstream

It's not a sign of who you were to me;
it's a sign of who you are:
no one that I know…
    anymore.

He's tall and sturdy like the oak
I carved our initials in,
but as time goes on
you either grow or wither down,
and like your eyes so richly brown…
into the dirt is where I'll take you
because *Spider's* only build webs
that the breath of rhyme could blow apart.

I walked in white,
unsoiled by a black cloud
that never opened up,
    or
the dirt of brown eyes
still wearing thin on me.
With his back to me,
I knew he saw more in me
    than just poetry.
He found an oak…
tall and sturdy enough to be…
      his wife
in all aspects of his life,
and I never had to carve a thing in me
      to feel permanent.

Heather Angelika Dooley

For once being in love with a fool,
    and being…
    a fool in love;
one that no longer picks up a pen.

For my reflective rhymes,
for looking for intangible signs,
for carving into my oak,
for having a scar that I can't deny…
for taking the chance again on

    love that never dies…

behind squints and lashes,
he said, "I do" to it all.

    Now I'm a blond,
    in all it's symbolism.

One in the Same

It's incredibly rare when you find a true friend.
It's incredibly rare when you find a true best love.
It's the rarest of them all when you find them both—
    fraternal twins
    in one set of bones.
You can forever not let one of them go for the other
because they share the same heart.

    Yours.

Sometimes the Quiet Ones Say the Most

I once lived with someone for one short year.
He was just a small-town boy
and I was already a woman.
He was too quiet,
and I fancied myself the wordy, worldly sort
(but I wasn't).
This is what ruined us.
I could just never understand him.

Yet, he once said to me,
"I hate people because…
I love them so much."

He never said a lot,
but when he did…

      he did.

Years have gone by.
We never spoke again
after we parted ways.
He's a grown man now and…
I am just a girl these days.

But, I can finally say
that I understand him

    now.

Heather Angelika Dooley

The Kiss I Use

My hand never folds on me

    like you did.

And, yet, your purpose,

the only thing I have left to compare

    nothing to.

I'm galloping with this lead

to overflow my head

as if her cowgirl's finally got her Indian.

I subsist with nil in my stream,

but one lone beam.

My lone bone ranger

keeping me from turning into ruins.

Ink Blot in a Poet's Bloodstream

I can't find myself

    when

it's on the creases of your laugh lines—

    a dead end ditch

graver than any blood or year…

those bleached teeth I won't forget

    to stain.

A birthday typhoon

pushing your crow's feet off my face—

cosmetically throwing off the stars

that will make my life align with grace.

I wonder how many flavors I can keep getting

    out of this one

        kiss…

I keep using

and *using*

over and over?

Heather Angelika Dooley

The blood running through this hand,

not even lukewarm—

gone wintry over time.

I should not have drank what I spilled

even sooner than too late

instead of swallowing bath water

out of desperation to quench this thirst for lead

and rain from a birthday typhoon

that's rising out of the flavor of the kiss I use

    and used

        over and over.

Root Words

The root word of compromise is:
Promise.

Sometimes in order to have a promise made to you,
you must break one you made to someone else.

This, regrettably, sometimes compromises your integrity.

We must determine how much worth
words with roots have…

Heather Angelika Dooley

Dot, Dot, Dot

I took you this morning

before I ate a bite

of Eve's apple,

and now I have a

heartache

from the only thing that ever

made me...

well...

a solid...

foundation—

a coating in my

underlining

notes

that I'm not feeling so well...

hungry anymore.

Ink Blot in a Poet's Bloodstream

I am more

evolving

into more of a fiend every day

that I am not taking you

this morning

very well

(with a),

heartache.

Heather Angelika Dooley

Upper Resuscitation Infection

We take a breath when we're starved and hungry.

We exhale when we have too much inside to handle.

There's a point in the middle

when we stop breathing;

that's where we're really living.

It's after we fulfilled our craving

    when empty,

and right before we're too full

    of ourselves.

Berlin Has Nothing On Us

You take photos of me when I'm not looking.

I take photos of you when I don't have to look.

A mental snapshot of the things that could never be forgotten—

I put you in a (full) frame

because you're a part of the (big) picture.

I hang us on the wall

because it's easier now…

than to break it down

…just to invite you in.

Honest Evidence

Listen to your photo albums more than your thoughts,

or the things they told you about yourself.

You've lived bigger than they'll let you remember

and better than even you have ever noticed.

As the saying goes, "Pictures are worth a thousand words,"

and someday you, and everyone else, will see

you did the best you could.

Your photo albums tell true stories—

not your critics or your demons or your guilt.

You can't fake intention.

There will be a day that your photo albums will

be a memoir of all your best faces and years.

So, love the moments of how hard you tried,

and not how hard you lived.

You lived as hard as you could,

and you played so much harder than you lied…

…to make sure you left behind the best mental photo montage

for those you loved more than yourself.

Heather Angelika Dooley

Going to Confession

It's the bane of every writer's existence
that they are haunted by their own stories.

How could it not be
     when...
their lives roam around
on ink stained tattoos in
libraries, independent bookstores,
and people's nightstands?

This is my church,
my cathedral,
my chapel,
my abbey.

     My basilica.

But, this is what it means to have words
live so large in you that you become
processed by them,
like angels and demons;
you have no other choice than to
     exorcise
        and exercise them—
          treadmill redemption
you can't mention unless it's considered art,
then you're exempt from outward judgment.

Ink Blot in a Poet's Bloodstream

Every day, I take my angels and demons out on a long run
just to drive them out of me
and onto the page.
They bleed out of me
and into something you
can shelf, always to know my story,
without ever having to really know

    me.

Words
are my religion
and your damna*tion*.

I wouldn't have it any other way,
or I wouldn't be who I am, not *holy*,
    at least.

Heather Angelika Dooley

Weathered Over Time

What happens when you take the first "T" from trust?

Finishing Last Isn't a Bad Thing

There are many things a man can do to make you love them.
There are just as many things a man can do
    to make you
    respect them.

Even though those things they do to make you love them
    make you fall hard,
without those things that make you respect them,
you might not get back up to see them eye to eye.

The best man makes you respect yourself
even more than you already did.

Respect isn't always romantic.
True love comes in so many forms—
the forms that don't let anyone finish last.

    May the best man always win.

Heather Angelika Dooley

Manner of the Love Chapel

My Grandma Jane used to always say,
"You know you're in love when he makes your heart sing
    when he comes around the corner."

I now sing like Billie Holiday and Pavarotti
when all that I ever could do before was…

    hum.

Enlarged Heart

Charles Bukowski once wrote,

"My Dear,
find what you love and let it kill you."

But, it isn't your vices that kill you…
it's what drives you to them.

And, it might just be what you love the most
that teaches you what your heart can't take.

First Snow

Sometimes the best words—

in spite of all the great big ones—

   are…

"I'm on my way home."

Come hang your hat, my love.

I may never put mine on

   …again.

Don't Let it Get Stuck on the Way Out

I never forget a face.
But, I never forget the sound a door makes
    as it closes, either.
        So,

one might not mean as much
        as one might think.

Lye Soap

I washed my hands of you today.

I can no longer see where you once held them.

Trapeze Artist—This Is My Arial Act

It takes some time to learn the ropes,

   but once you do…

you're no longer a noose around the neck,

   dangling in midair.

Heather Angelika Dooley

Back Pocket

So, I am getting ready to publish another book.
I remember when I read you Merrit's poems
in that apartment off of McNab Avenue,
the one with a mattress on the cold tile floor
and the fake streetlight moonlight streaming through the
    vertical blinds—
as we laid horizontal, collecting our own light.
You would grab my handwritten poetry and say,
"Let me recite the next great poet…"
and you read me everything I had written you.
You said, "One day, you will have as many books as her;
you're going to write your way into everyone's hearts
    like you have mine."

You believed in me.
I have kept that in my front pocket
every time life put me in it's back one.

There are so many days I doubt everything that I did—
every decision that I made after us along the way,
but late at night when I am lonely,
    fulfilled,
    disappointed,
    enchanted,
scared what the future brings,
and looking forward to it…

Ink Blot in a Poet's Bloodstream

I think about how you believed in me,
and how Merrit wrote my forward for MY book;
how she and I became friends
like you and I only daydreamed about,
and now I talk to Molly sometimes,
when she was once just a picture in a book
that we looked at as we planned our own family.
While you read me my poetry through a vertical blind
    with fake streetlight moonlight,
and you told me that I could write books too—
me never believing that I would ever meet my muse,
but being certain that we'd be writing all of the stories.

That did not happen because it was not supposed to, but…

I needed you to help me put all of these books together.
Even if you ended up not being in most of them,
    I still wrote them,
      just like you said I would.
      I kept that in my back pocket
as I wrote about what was in my front one,

    every day since.

It's sometimes hard to believe that it wasn't you,
but it doesn't mean that you weren't my biggest believer.
You ended up being the back pocket.
That still means something;
it just did not turn out to be everything we thought it would,
but look at what happened! Neither of us would have ever truly believed

that I would be sending MY poetry to Merrit—
not even we believed that would happen.
And you and I believed in anything,
so that says everything about the kind of
dreamer you believed that I was.

No matter what…
no matter how old I get and how many books I publish,
I always reread them on that mattress in the apartment
off of McNab Avenue on the cold tile floor with the streetlight moonlight
coming through the vertical blinds,
because I know that you were the only one that believed
    that I would do this—
    even more than me.

Now it's just me. And poetry. A fourth book. And time. And…

    full back pockets.

Two kids daydreaming turned into this.
    I did it.

    I,

    clearly,

believed in you, too.

Dear John Done,

I feel like I need to write you a thank you note

for hurting me more than anyone else ever has.

When you gave me my heart back,

you were the heartless one, then.

But, I have to thank you so much.

Now it is impossible to take anything for granted.

I didn't know I could ever love like this!

You said, "Look at you, you're so beautiful…

You're going to find someone better so soon."

Right then, it was hard to believe anything you said.

Now, I thank you with every fiber of my being.

Thank you for hurting me more than anyone else ever has.

I can't thank you enough, again,

for giving me the gift of being the happiest that I've ever been.

Heather Angelika Dooley

It was the nicest thing you ever did for me—

being heartless.

Sincerely,
Free Bird

Make Love to Your Life

In took me 28 years to write all of these poems in this book.
In the next 28 years, I will probably be dead.
I am more than halfway through my life already.
When I read these poems, I am right back there like it was yesterday.
    Life is so fresh.
    Life is so real.
    Life is so vivid.
I don't care what anyone says;
the life of an artist never ages.
We were old the day that we were born.
But, the beauty of us is also that we never get old—
we live deep in each colorful memory.

I love it that I am going to get old as I write about youth,
and I love it that I stay young writing about growth,
but let's be real…

Life goes by so fast.
28 years ago was a blink,
and just when you think you have time to plan for the next chapter,
you're already in it,
and then in it again,
and again.

Write it all down.
Take pictures of it all.
Paint it.
Draw it.
Sing it.
Dance it.
Drink it.
Hug it.
Kiss it.
Grab it.
Build it.
Travel to it.
Love the hell out of it.

Make love to your life now,
because 28 years ago I wrote the first poem in this book
and I am just getting around to publishing it now.

I am still holding hands with the girl that wrote that poem;
    she is still me.
    But, I am no longer her.
    Life has changed me,
    and again,
    and again.

I am halfway through my life now.
That girl will never meet me in another 28 years.
That's not a long time, you guys.
It's a hard celebration knowing she will never know
herself at the moment she dies.

Ink Blot in a Poet's Bloodstream

So, say your hellos and goodbyes
   every day
   by making love to your life.

Don't wait for it to make love to you;
it goes by in a blink.

Heather Angelika Dooley

Let's Just Get This Out of the Way Now

I'm a lover,
not a fighter,
so don't start crap with me;
you'll never win.

I have been through enough in my 39 years.

That's what makes me tough
      as nails.

I will roundhouse kick,
sucker punch,
and *overhand* you up with my raging love.

It is what I am best at.
My heart does not go down without the good fight;
I love unconditionally with all of my might.

I fight for love with my whole soft heart,
and a whole lot of laughter in the hard times.

I will fight so hard
to make things easy.

The Vow To My Next Book
(April 25, 2014)

I, Heather Angelika Dooley,

take you, Sean Donal Pecor,

to be my beyond lawfully wedded husband.

I take you to have and to hold,

for better or for worse, for richer, for poorer, in sickness and in health,

to love and to cherish, from this day forward until death do us part.

I do this because you're my best friend, my family, the person I knew I'd always find,

and my end all/be all.

I will stop at nothing to be your soldier,

your lover,

and your confidant.

No matter what comes way for us,

I will rally,

because I cherish you,

and have adored you from the genesis of us…

and I'm your girl, always.

I met you and you made the difference.

I will stop at nothing to be in your corner.

Until the day we die, you have me on your side.

I'm the one who has it in her to arrive,

for I believe you deserve all the love I have to give you, and you to give to me—

it's more than I ever knew I encompassed.

I love you today; I love you tomorrow, and I'll love you into eternity.

I don't know where you end and where I begin.

Let's do this! Forever.

It's you and me against the world, my love.